Steps to Self-Editing

Jana S. Brown

Opal Kingdom Press

Copyright 2023 Opal Kingdom Press

Print ISBN- 978-1-952415-11-1

Ebook ISBN – 978-1-952415-12-8

Cover Design by: Melissa McShane

First Printing

10 9 8 7 6 5 4 3 2 1

Dedicated to Melissa who provided welcome encouragement and a large box of commas.

Contents

Introduction and Notes from the Author

WHO AM I?

My name is Jana S. Brown. I'm an author, editor, presenter, teacher, and book marketer. I've been involved in writing and publishing for over 25 years. Okay, so it's coming on 30, but what's five years, more or less? At this point in my career, I publish under three pennames in a variety of genres, and I love them all. I work in book marketing, and I love teaching courses around writing and publishing. There is nothing quite as satisfying as seeing a fellow author learn and succeed!

Why this book?

My first experiences with being an editor go back to high school, where I was a member of the yearbook team and we were required to exchange yearbook articles and edit for each other. Even back then, it was obvious there was a big difference between working on the articles that had been self-edited and the ones that were still rough drafts. Over the years, my editing experience has expanded on both sides of the pen. I've become much better at editing my own work (not that I would skip professional editing to back me up) and learned to identify issues that I see over and over again as an editor across client manuscripts.

I firmly believe that authors will have a better experience with their editors if they are coming to the party with a manuscript that has been self-edited. The experience is so much more positive, and due to the fact that most editors charge by the word, authors with a tightly self-edited book will save money on their edits! Who doesn't want to do that?

In this book we will talk about the types of self-editing: developmental, line, and copy. If you notice those echo the kind of editing the pros do, there's a reason or three for that. Your self-editing is a microcosm of that bigger editing process, and time spent learning how these edits tie together is never wasted.

All of the information in this book will be as correct as I can make it as of 2023. I'll update the content as often as it makes sense to.

As well, there is a glossary of editing and publishing terms and definitions at the end of the book, so you have a fast reference for anything you don't remember.

Now, as I've said before, pull up a virtual seat at my table, drinks are in the fridge and cookies on the counter.

Let's get down to business.

Why Do We Need Editing, and What Is It?

THERE ARE MANY CAMPS when it comes to the definition of editing and its purpose, and those camps feel strongly about their positions. For the purpose of *this* book, the definition of editing is: the process of taking a draft of a manuscript and cleaning it up in terms of structure, clarity and detail, continuity, and grammar to prepare it for publication and sales. This cleaning up is done based on standardized expectations for storytelling and grammatical accuracy. At its heart, editing is about making sure the words you've written don't get in the way of the story you're telling.

So what editing is seems pretty straightforward. This leads to the bigger question: why do we need it?

Many writers over the ages have wrestled with this question. After all, the writer has written his or her work in exactly the way they intended. If someone else steps toe in it, is it truly the same work? It's a very existential question, and not the one I'm most interested in answering.

The reason we need editing, in my opinion, is much more straightforward. The process of writing and reading is basically one of mind control. A writer (you) creates a story expressed by little black marks on a blank page. A reader translates those little black marks from the page into their mind. If both parts of this relationship have gone well, then the reader's mind sees what the writer's mind imagined and expressed. Editing is about making that relationship as seamless as possible. To take control of a reader's mind, there can't be anything in the creation and display of the words themselves or how they are put together that drives the reader out of the narrative. When a reader encounters grammatical errors, awkward phrasing, contradictions, and plots that bring no satisfaction, they are driven from the narrative and may not return for another one. These issues are like bumps on a ski slope. Readers can handle a few of them, and – at times – they might even be unique and exhilarating, but too many bumps and the thrill turns into terror and retirement from the slope. Editing smooths the reader's path and enhances the writer's intention to create the best possible experience and return.

Lest you protest that the analogy only works for fiction, it applies to non-fiction as well. Non-fiction that is badly organized, that contains logical loops or incorrect and conflicting information, will also drive the reader away. In both cases, editing can help identify and address these flaws.

From a functional point of view, editing is also about making a work able to be sold. Manuscripts that are published with a plethora (that's such a fun word, plethora!) of errors will not pass review on the various distribution platforms, and if they are, readers will have no problem pointing out all of the issues in their reviews or in email. Both are rather disheartening and can hurt sales. If enough errors are reported to the distribution platforms, a manuscript will be removed all together.

If you are approaching traditional publishing, a manuscript that is very rough will have a hard time finding a place with an agent or an acquisitions editor. They want to see your work at its very best, even if the publisher may apply additional editing and house style guides to the finished product. If two books alike in all other ways come to an editor's desk, but one is well edited and easy to read, and the other has glaring, basic errors, the first book will win the day, as much less work will be required to take it to market.

A clean, easy to read manuscript with solid structure and satisfying characters and plot arcs bridges that gap to the reader and convinces them to trust in your skill and return to buy more books from you.

A note about what editing should NOT do: Editing should never be a slavish adherence to grammatical rules without thought as to context and intention. Any editing software can accomplish that (and can be useful in this process). However, such adherence will generally remove the unique value of the author's voice and experience. In many cases, voice and author intention will, and should, trump a grammatical rule. This is double the case when it comes to dialogue, which breaks the rules because people rarely speak in a grammatically accurate fashion. Editing should also not place the opinion of the editor over the author, but each suggestion should be considered and pondered and if it makes the *work* better or brings clarity, it should be put in place. If it doesn't, it should be abandoned. The editor is not there to rewrite the work as they would have done it, but to help scrub off the rough edges and make the work more what the author envisions and the audience expects.

Editing Within the Publishing Process

KNOWING WHAT EDITING IS leads to another question, that of where editing fits in within the publishing process. It's a good question, and various types of editing show up in various places. So, let's take a look at the process in broad strokes.

In self-publishing, the process is as follows:

- Manuscript creation

- Self-Editing

- Beta Readers

- Professional Editing

- Formatting

- Cover Design

- Proofreading

- Publication

Some authors switch up beta reading and professional editing and others swap formatting and proofreading. Whichever way works for your process is fine, but you should have a process.

You can see at least three points of editing in this process. Let's define those points.

Self-editing is the process of the author applying corrections to the manuscript.

Professional editing is bringing in an expert to edit the manuscript.

Proofreading is a last pair of eyes on the manuscript to search for any stray typos or formatting errors.

In traditional publishing, the process is a little more complex:

- Manuscript creation

- Self-Editing

- Beta Readers

- Agent Query and Acceptance

- Acquiring Editor Query and Acceptance

- Professional Editing by the publishing house

- Formatting by the publishing house

- Proofreading – Usually the author will be given a copy of their work, called galleys, to review for errors. Some publishing houses will have a final proofreader on staff at this point as well, but it varies from house to house.

- Publication

While editing comes into this process at least three times, do not think that this means that every single potential error or fat-fingered typo will be found. Typos are pernicious and devious and a few will slip by even the most eagle-eyed of editing professionals. This happens both in the self-publishing and traditional sphere. (I own a copy of a traditionally published book where there is an entire section of the book where the letters pi were all replaced by the mathematical symbol π. So the symbol is in the middle of words and in funny places on the page. No matter who you are, the typo or weird glitch gremlins can get you.) Fortunately, if you are self-publishing, it is easy to fix typos even after the manuscript has gone live. In the case of traditional publishing, your publisher may be willing to fix errors on future print runs.

Do the best you can, and then engage your inner zen and move onto the next project.

Types of Editing

NOW THAT WE'VE TALKED the what and the why of editing, let's get into the process and application. When it comes to the actual process, editing can be broken down into three different categories. There are sometimes different names for these categories in the publishing industry, but the functions are the same. In both self-editing and professional editing each of these types should be completed. We'll get down to exactly *how* to pursue each in future chapters, but let's set some groundwork here.

1: Developmental or Structural Editing

Developmental editing is the process of looking at the manuscript from the viewpoint of the larger structure. If we were to compare editing to building a house, the developmental edits make sure the book has a solid foundation and walls. They make sure the trusses of character arc and development are solid and there is a logical and contextual flow to the plot and story resolution. In non-fiction, these edits can include fact checking and making sure the book is structured in a fashion that makes sense and builds on the central problem being solved or the education being offered. Non-fiction is generally written to educate and solve problems. Fiction is generally written to entertain. (There is certainly cross-over, but let's keep it simple, shall we?)

2: Line or Style Editing

Line editing is the process of looking at the manuscript from the viewpoint of author style, voice, clarity, and continuity. In our analogy of the house, the line editing makes sure the style of the house looks good and matches throughout, gardens of nicely flowing paragraphs are placed where they won't get trampled, and the various shades of descriptive paint are co-ordinated to best effect. When line editing, you are looking to remove repetition and awkwardness and address continuity and voice.

3: Copy or Mechanical Editing

Copy editing is the process of looking at the manuscript from the view-point of the technical correctness of the grammar and mechanics of lan-guage, including proper spelling, hyphenation, word choice, punctuation, etc. Returning to the analogy, the copy editing is the finishing touches to the home, from straightening the photos on the wall to buffing out the paint strokes on the door.

You can see how all three of these types of editing work together to create a complete editing house, and a clean, clear manuscript.

Tools for Self-Editing

IN ORDER TO CREATE our editing house, let's review some of the tools you can use to make the self-editing process straight forward and repeatable. As you'll be self-editing every book you write, the better your tools and personal process are (this comes with practice) the easier it will be.

1: A standard dictionary. Most commonly, authors select between the *Merriam-Webster Dictionary* and the *Oxford English Dictionary*. These are both solid resources. It is best to choose one dictionary and stick with it, as there are differences between the two, particularly when it comes to rules which are handled differently between American English and British English. It does not matter which one you use, but consistency is king when it comes to any type of editing, and consistency in use requires having a consistent source.

2: A good basic grammar guide. This may be a hard copy guide, or an online resource, but again look for a consistent one or maybe two sources to lean on. Personally, I'm a big fan of Grammar Girl online, though I also keep a copy of *Conan the Grammarian* on hand as a fun resource that is also good for holding off the fantasy hordes.

3: In the case of non-fiction (which we won't go into extensively, but I'm not going to ignore it either), a copy of the standard APA, MLA, or other professional guidelines appropriate to your publication. This is important because your work should be standard for your field of non-fiction. These standards give information on things like how a referenced work should be cited and listed in a bibliography, abbreviations, and other technical use standards.

4: A style guide. This is something you will need to create for yourself, though you can find a number of templates for one online, including at my website (www.geekgirlsacademy.com). A style guide is your reference for rules within your book and series that need to be consistent, even if they fly in the face of traditional formatting or grammar. An example might be a word that generally is not capitalized being used as a political position within the world and thus treated as a proper noun, or how you are going to format a texting interaction, as there isn't a generalized standard for that. These guides are helpful in self-editing and should be shared when you hire a professional editor so that the editor does not helpfully mark up issues that you have determined will be non-standard.

5: Editorial software. In the last several years, more and more software options to help with editing have been created. Some of these are good, and some of them... well... not so good. Make sure to do appropriate research before signing up for any of these programs or apps and remember that these are computer editors. They will give you a very technical edit, but they are not good at discerning when context or voice should be favored over technical correctness. If you use any of these options, you should never just accept all changes. Just like when getting edits from a human editor, you should review each edit and decide if it is correct for this particular book or not, and only accept the ones that work. If in doubt, strike the correction and ask an expert for advice.

Software examples:

- MS Word spellcheck (I don't really recommend their grammar check. It is occasionally correct, but it's more often not.)

- Grammarly Pro

- Pro Writing Aid

- Hemmingway App

- ChatGPT/other AI assistants

Be aware of the costs of the software as well. Sometimes you are charged once, sometimes yearly, and sometimes monthly. Make sure you are getting enough value out of the software to have a good return on investment for that charge.

6: Style manuals. Here I am going to lean away from what many self-editing books suggest and say that, with the exception of the non-fiction manuals, authors generally do not need to own their own style manual such as *The Chicago Manual of Style*. It certainly doesn't *hurt* to have a copy. I have the last several editions, but that's because I am an editor for others and a word nerd. If you want a copy, it's a fantastic reference, but most professional editors will probably have a copy and can do that level of checking for you during their editing pass.

7: A sense of humor, and knowing when to accept that done is better than perfect. Many authors hate the process of revision and edit only reluctantly, accepting it as a necessary part of publishing. This isn't unreasonable as editing isn't always the fun part. This is why you need to have grace and humor as part of your editing toolkit, and also why you need to put perfectionism aside. In the same way that using tools that don't understand an author voice can remove the passion from the work, so can overediting. I know of authors who go over a draft ten or fifteen or even twenty times, and they get so frustrated because it seems like it's getting worse and not better, and that's true. They are trying so hard for perfection that they are chopping their book to bits and losing the passion it was created with in the first place.

In my opinion, unless you've made an extreme change, your work needs less than five revisions, even better if it's less than three, before it moves on to a professional editor who can help you bring it home. Particularly if you are looking at publishing as a career, you must get material out into the public, and waiting on perfectionism will keep this from happen. Truly, sometimes perfect is the enemy of done (you'll hear this phrase again later), and there will be times you can do nothing more with the manuscript in front of you and you need to continue learning and growing with a new book.

Planning Your Self-Editing and When to Start

WHEN IT COMES TO self-editing, one of the discussions I see frequently is the argument over whether you should self-edit as you go, or should wait until the manuscript is complete before editing begins. There are pros and cons to both of these methods.

Self-editing As You Go

Self-editing as you go is often called cycling, and is just what it sounds like. You create a section of the manuscript and then go back and apply editing before moving on to the next section. In the best cases, this method creates a very clean first draft and eliminates a lot of rewriting since you can make corrections in the flow of the manuscript at the time of creation. Many experienced authors prefer this method so they don't spend as much time on edits. The downfall of this method is when it slows the process of moving forward and creating. Some authors will write a first chapter, then edit it, then edit it again, then again, and then... You get the idea. If editing as you go is keeping you from *going* then don't do it. You can leave all of the edits for the end.

Some pantsers – authors who write into the dark or by the seat of their pants – struggle with cycling in edits because it breaks their rhythm of moving forward to go back to older tex. It's fine if this is you, just expect and plan for a longer editing period after the rough draft is complete.

Self-editing After Manuscript Completion

Self-editing after manuscript completion is just what it sounds like and is often called a full revision. This consists of putting off all editing, except maybe minor typos, until the manuscript is written. This method is suggested by the folks at NaNoWriMo and a lot of authors who need to get the words out of their heads before making sure they are the right words. The quote I see most often about this is allowing yourself to "write a shitty rough draft as long as you write it." Waiting for edits can help you avoid analysis paralysis that might derail your progress, particularly if you are a fast writer.

The con of waiting is that if you've made a major error in continuity or plotting, it can mean a LOT of rewriting to go back and fix everything all the way through a completed manuscript. The weight of correcting these problems can kill a project, because it is finished, but the amount of work required to make it both finished *and* publishable is high, and you may already be enthusiastic about a new project. In this case, you may choose to do less self-editing, knowing that it will mean paying a professional more to do the work for you. I still think you will benefit from taking at least one walk through and fixing everything you can before taking that next step.

So, part of my message here is that neither of these methods for addressing self-edits is perfect for everyone, but you need to figure out which one works for you in your process right now. The "right now" is important because your process will change over time, and you may find that you start with one method and shift to the other, or something in between. As long as you know what self-editing requires from you so you can plan enough time to do it, then you're doing it right.

Let's Get Into the Nuts and Bolts

Now that we've defined what self-editing is, why you need it, what you need to prepare yourself, and when to do it, we're going to spend the rest of this book digging into the how. I'll break out each of the three levels of editing and review, what you need to be looking for, ways to find and correct it, and supply some handy tips and tricks. If you're just starting on your publishing journey, these lists are going to look huge and overwhelming. (I'm not just starting and sometimes they look huge and overwhelming to me, too! You're in good company.) Just take things one step at a time. This process will get better with each book, and that's okay.

One other thing before we start is that I want you to get very comfortable with the phrase "search and consider" instead of "search and replace". There are multiple reasons for this distinction, starting with the fact there are always exceptions to the rule. Sometimes you will choose to do something grammatically incorrect because it works for your author voice, or it's in dialogue and you are trying to capture a certain type of speech. If you merely search and replace, you may change out things you want to keep. As well, search and replace is... well... very literal. I am reminded of a story from a fellow editor who was working on a project after an author had completed his self-edit. In the self-editing process, the author had decided that all references to pants would now be trousers and made a global search and replace. This became a point of giggles when every reference to occupants were now occutrousers.

So, search, consider, and choose your usage. This is a good time to build or add to your personal style guide for your book and/or series. Mark down the things you choose to do consistently that may go against expectations, and when you turn your manuscript to your professional editor give them the style guide and they won't go changing your occutrousers back to occupants if that's truly what you want.

Developmental or Structural Editing

WHEN YOU LOOK AT a novel (this works for shorter works too) from a structural point of view there are several parts to consider.

1. Overall story structure

2. Plot and character development

3. Promises and foreshadowing

4. Scenes and chapter structure

5. Pacing and tension

6. Plot holes and continuity

7. Point of view and tense

Let's break these down into bite-sized chunks.

Overall Story Structure

When it comes to story structure, there are a number of different systems, beat sheets, and other guides you can use. I'm not going to try to touch on all of them (or even any of them) here, but instead we'll focus on six aspects of high-level story structure you need to make sure work together throughout your manuscript to create a satisfying reader experience. Remember that for each genre, the expectations for what happens or how these pieces of structure come together may be slightly different. The best research you can do to learn these expectations is to read widely—both in your genre and out—and watch what readers and reviews say about the best and top selling books.

- **Establishing the normal.** This is generally an opening section, or sometimes a prologue (No, prologue is not a dirty word. They just have to be used carefully) where you establish what is normal for the character(s) and the world. Some books jump past this to begin with the inciting incident or in medias res – the middle of the action– and then loop back to the establishing shot. Either way can work, but read in your genre so you know the conventions. Establishment usually doesn't take long, and should not just be a long info dump of backstory. A good example would be how many romance books give each of the main romantic interests one chapter to say where they are now before they meet. For example: Joan is running a diner in small town Texas and loves her life. Fred is a high-powered business executive on his way to that same small town to decide if his company can drill for oil. This example would be written out into one or two chapters with fun details to establish who they both are, where they are in their lives, and put them on a collision course for trouble.

- **The hook or inciting incident**. This is the event or moment that sets the story in motion. It should be something relevant to the main character, or main plot, or both, that creates a problem or a challenge for the protagonist. (The main character and protagonist are generally the same character, and I use these terms interchangeably even knowing there are exceptions). It will be something or someone that comes into the protagonist's life and changes their circumstance, or stands in the way of the protagonist getting what they want or what they need, even if that need is as simple as survival! The inciting incident should generally occur within the first 10-20% of your novel. There are, as always, exceptions to this rule, as some genres will tolerate a very slow start, but for the most part, the hook is what pulls the reader in and lets them know the stakes of a story. If it takes too long to get the story rolling, they will get bored and put the book down. I always get at least one person who points to a 'classic' book as an example of a very slow start (Ernest Hemingway, anyone?) and why can't they do that? Don't compare yourselves to the classics, folks. In many cases, books that we consider classics would not be picked up for publication by modern publishing houses or readers. They have styles that are appropriate to their time and stand on their laurels. You aren't writing in that time or for that audience. It benefits you to learn from what they've done, but apply the strategies that work now.

- **Rising action**. This is the part of the story where the protagonist faces obstacles and challenges that stand in the way of their goal. Through this section, there should be high points of emotional tension and lower points and moments of intense action set off by dialogue and discovery. Each obstacle should lead to the next, with the obstacles becoming more and more difficult to overcome. Sometimes over the course of the rising action, the nature of what the protagonist wants and needs will change because of the trials they face. For example: Initially your reluctant hero may just want to take the McGuffin to the nearest smart guy and get rid of it because his goal/want is to go back home and marry the girl and raise fat babies. However, during the course of the rising action, the reluctant hero may come to realize that the bigger quest requires his participation in order to keep his people at peace so there is a home to return to. He thus engages with the quest on a personal level, and now his need to save his people is bigger than his want of going home. He needs to succeed in the quest and then maybe go home. Or maybe by that point he will decide to live in the bigger world because of the changes he has faced. We'll talk about this more during character arcs, but it's a good idea to wrap your brain around now. Interesting characters change, the rising action is where they do a lot of that changing, or at least where the set up for change occurs.

- **Climax.** This is the pivotal turning point of the story, the thing all that rising action has been building to, where the protagonist faces their biggest challenge and makes a decision or take an action that determines the outcome of the story. The climax should be the most dramatic and intense moment in the book, but that is not to say it is always the most positive moment in the book. Pay close attention to the term "turning point." In different genres, the expectations of this turning point may be different. For example, in fantasy the climax very often is literally a battle where a great evil is faced and defeated. In mystery, the climax is when all the clues come together and resolution revealed. For romance, the climax is often when love looks like it is lost, a big break up followed by a resolution to fix that dark moment. Depending on the genre, sometimes the climax isn't vastly dramatic, but unless you are writing something like a travel log or memoir, the climax needs to be there. Readers look for and anticipate this turning point. It's part of what they are cheering for, or dreading, and without it, you miss a critical emotional beat and your story will not be satisfying.

- **Falling Action**. This is the part of the story where the consequences of the climax are revealed and loose ends are tied up. The tension eases through this section, setting up closure for the reader and the ending. In ongoing series, some loose ends are left to carry the reader forward, but enough of the plot threads are closed that the reader feels satisfied by what has happened and been resolved in this book, and anxious to read on to the next one. You can use a cliffhanger where the resolution is uncertain or doesn't occur, but use those judiciously as many readers dislike them.

- **Resolution**. This is the end of the story, where anything else that needs to be resolved is settled, and the protagonist reaches their goal or reaches the next step that will lead them to their goal in the next story. In general, there will be a sense of closure on the current issues, even if there are bigger events across the series that are still being addressed. When you have a final book in a series, the falling action and resolution may draw out longer than in previous books, depending on how many active characters you've introduced. In something like epic fantasy, the resolution may take a while, as these tend to be large multi-POV worlds and readers want closure for the majority of their new character friends. The resolution draws the last of the threads together and puts a bow on the book.

So now that you know what the parts are, what are you supposed to do with that when you are self-editing? Break your book down into those parts. Make sure they are all there, and make sure each part is accomplishing what it's supposed to. If you can't identify an inciting incident, or a climax, or the book wanders off in resolution for a dozen chapters after the climax, then you need to trim and tighten, or you may need to go back in and add chapters or a subplot.

Still confused? Let's take apart a classic fairy tale as an example. I'm going to use Cinderella here. Yes, I know there are a million versions of

Cinderella, but they generally follow a form and that'll work for what we are talking about.

Cinderella

- Setting the normal – Cinderella has lost her parents and lives with her stepmother and stepsiblings. The relationship between Cinderella and the rest of her family is not good, though she may have friends in the form of servants or animal companions. Her role in the household is that of servant and while she doesn't like her life, she remains hopeful for change.

- Hook or inciting incident – The prince is having a ball! Word comes to the household about the event and Cinderella wants to go.

- Rising action – Cinderella works hard to help her stepsiblings prepare for the ball (admittedly because she has to), but also works toward ways that she can go herself. In most versions of Cinderella, working with the godmother to create appropriate footwear and a ride to the ball is all part of the rising action. Going to the ball is still rising action. It is taking the main character to the point where the climax of the story can happen.

- Climax – The climax of the story begins when she meets the prince at the ball and things seem to be going well. It hits the highest point when the clock strikes midnight, and she makes a dash for it leaving behind her fashionable footwear.

- Falling action – The prince, duke, whoever is in charge of the search, goes from house to house trying the shoe on the eligible. Eventually, Cinderella is found to have the perfect size foot (though I prefer the versions where there's a little magic involved and the shoe won't fit anyone that isn't her, no matter the size of the tootsies). Depending on the version, this may also be where the stepfamily makes amends or is punished for their actions over the years.

- Resolution – Cinderella is brought to the castle, and takes up a new life as a princess (Or she decides to open a shoe shop because princessing isn't as fun as it's cracked up to be). Happily ever after.

You can see from this example that there are places where the separation between the sections is very distinct. In other places they wander all over each other, and that's okay. As long as you can still tell that everything is there and is accomplishing the correct purpose, you've got the structure in place.

Now, you may have noticed that I haven't talked about having this structure in place before you start writing. It helps to make your self-editing cleaner if you have a high-level outline of these structure points from the beginning, but if that's not the way you work, it's okay. You do need to make sure the structure is there in the end. This basic story structure (often known as the plot mountain or story mountain) is a classic structure that readers expect, and if you're missing a major point, or each part isn't achieving what it's there for, you'll get reader complaints. They may not be able to identify you waited too long or glossed over the inciting incident, for example, but they will say things like: "This book started so slowly." "I was bored." "It took forever for anything important to happen." So, learn to read like a reader and break your book down to make sure it hits those points.

If you are struggling to create this break down on your own, there are software options such as Plottr There are also other structure guides that break these points down into more beats or acts, or have a different shape to the structure, etc., etc. I'll put a list of resources in the index if you'd like to branch out. But in the end, almost all of these ways of getting at structure will still overlap this basic six-point form. This is a good place to start, and if you have this foundation in place, the rest of your self-edits will build upon it.

Plot and Character Development

When it comes to plot and character development, there's plenty of advice on how to address them. For some folks, it's all about pulling them apart and looking only at plot aspects and then at the character aspects. In my opinion, these two things are usually tightly woven together, and when you are in self-editing mode it's important to be able to look at the whole and make sure it all works together. You may have to pull plot and character apart to figure out how you want to fix problems, but let's start with identifying five things you'll want to watch for when it comes to your characters and your plot.

- **Consistent and evolving characterization**. Examine your characters to ensure that their characterization remains consistent. This is not the point where you are searching for details about their clothing staying the same, but about the deeper character. If they love dogs at the beginning, do we see that touched on throughout? Are they working toward their goals and desires? If they fail, how are they working to overcome the failure? If their goals and desires change, do the changes make sense given their experiences? Characters should experience growth and change over the course of the book. They will experience conflict, and this should deepen their development and provide space for action and reaction that makes sense for who they are and what they want. Major shifts in character traits, beliefs, or behaviors should make sense and be rational for their experiences. If a shift happens and there isn't a reason for it, the readers will be confused. So let your characters evolve and grow, but never forget who they are and where they came from. All of these things inform who they become.

- **Motivations and goals**. I mentioned this above, but it's important enough to look at in its own point. Review the motivations and goals of your main characters. Are they clearly defined and believable? The most relatable characters have strong desires that drive their actions, decision making process, and interactions with others. These desires may mature or change through the book, but that process of change should make sense based on where they start, their wants and needs, and the events and people they encounter.

- **Conflict and obstacles**. Make sure that your plot provides conflict and obstacles for your characters to overcome. It is often said, and I agree, that there is no story without conflict, at least not an interesting one. Now, when I say conflict, that doesn't always mean physical confrontations, or battles, or even arguments. Conflict is simply something that is getting in the way of the main character getting what they want. A simple example: If my daughter asks me for a treat, I may say "no". I am thwarting what she wants. Her desire to get a treat remains unchanged, but she has to look for other ways to get it. This may turn into a negotiation to have a treat, but only after her room is clean—an obstacle to overcome. Or it may turn into her sneaking a treat, and bearing the repercussions if (when) she is caught. Or she may decide that she doesn't really want a treat strongly enough to keep pursuing it, and her goal will now be to go outside and play. These are all examples of how her pursuit of a treat can be an interesting story. If she asks for a treat and I shrug and say "sure", that's not much of a story worth telling. Without conflict, even one as minor as making a request and having it denied, it's just an event, not a story.

- **Relationships and interactions**. Take a look at the relationships between your characters. Are these relationships sensible? Are they compelling and nuanced? Will the reader believe these characters are siblings, or are romantically interested in each other, or they loathe each other? Do their words and actions underline and express their true feelings? If they are hiding their true feelings, are they successful? Look for opportunities to deepen relationships, reveal hidden feelings and backstory, and create tension through dialogue, actions, and interactions. This is another area where genre comes into play strongly. There are genres where the character arcs pretty much are the plot. A lot of women's fiction is like this. Those are books about a woman's journey and self-discovery, so her relationships are primary aspects of both her character journey and the plot. In contrast, something like hard science fiction may not go as deeply into the character relationships, as the focus is on the plot and the technology. Make the relationships make sense for your genre, and within those constraints make sure we believe how the characters come together. Remember that relationship doesn't necessarily mean romance. You can have a book with no romance, but instead develop relationship dynamics in a family, or band of brothers, or strangers looking to survive the zombie apocalypse.

- **Emotional engagement**. Does your book create an emotional response in the reader? We should cheer for your characters when things are going well, and ache for them when they fail. Make sure there are highs and lows, that there are triumphs and setbacks all of which connect the reader to the plot and carry them to the resolution!

Reinforcing and highlighting these aspects of character and plot creates a more engaging and impactful story. Remember the goal is to keep your readers so immersed that they don't come up for air until the book is over and they are ready for the next one! Remember as you look at each of these editing steps, both the specific issues above and the ones we've talked about before and will talk about as we go, that each part connects to the others to create a cohesive and engaging whole.

Scene and Chapter Structure

So, you have a plot in place, the basic story structure is strong, and the characters have engaging arcs and emotional punch. The next part of structural editing is looking at the way the book is presented in terms of scene and chapter structure. This is a subject that you will hear a lot of questions about and arguments over. How long should a chapter be? is one of the questions I hear the most from my editing clients, and the answer is, as long as it needs to be. The purpose of a chapter is to create a moment in time and place where something is going to happen. A chapter may consist of one scene, or multiple scenes (or, in the case of Terry Pratchett, the entire book) but it usually ends at the point where the action shifts places or time or when the narrative moves on to a new plot point or beat. Most chapters mimic the format of a book. They introduce a subject, rise to a pivotal point, and then resolve, but this resolution needs to lead right into the next chapter. If it is too tied up in a bow, the chapter ending gives a reader a good place to put the book down and maybe forget to pick it up again.

Cliffhangers at the end of a book may annoy readers, but mini-cliffhangers at the end of chapters can push them on to read "just a little longer."

Scenes are smaller sections within a chapter. Some chapters are one long scene. Some chapters may have several closely related scenes broken up by locations, action beats, or by point of view. For example, in a romance, you may have an introductory scene where the two romantic interests are both going to a fair. The chapter may start with a scene in the point of view of one lead, showing his actions, thoughts, and the progression of the chapter arc. This may then have a scene break to shift into the point of view of the second main character and complete the chapter with her actions, thoughts, and the closing of the chapter arc. Using scenes in this fashion can help you to avoid confusion while allowing for information from both characters to be worked into the chapter.

Given all of that, how do you analyze if your chapters and scenes are working?

- Look for a clear purpose for each chapter. Does the chapter advance the plot, develop the characters, and/or provide important information? Most chapters will do some combination of the three. Avoid or remove chapters or scenes that are long infodumps of backstory, worldbuilding details, or navel gazing (where the view point character just sits back and ponders their situation). While pieces of this can be under the umbrella of important information, dumping everything someone needs to know about the world in one place is heavy handed and most readers will skip over the infodump and then be confused later.

- Take a good look at your transitions. What is a transition? It's the movement between scenes within a chapter and from one chapter to the next, even sometimes from one paragraph to the next. Smooth transitions help the book to flow and keep readers engaged. Good transitions follow a logical progression through the scenes and chapters in terms of both plot and emotional continuity. Transitions should avoid abrupt shifts in time, location, or perspective, unless those shifts are being intentionally used for dramatic effect. Now, a critical thing I see from authors who are trying to keep the transition from being abrupt is going too far the other way and describing every step a character takes from one location to the next or every event of a day when the most important things happen in the evening. A scene break – usually a large space or a decorative break – is often the easiest way to create a transition if there is a big change in setting from one section of the chapter to the next.

- Pace and tension. We'll get into this in detail in the next section, but how you structure your chapters and scenes also tie into the pacing of the book. Longer chapters read more slowly and can thus slow the pace of the narrative. In contrast, shorter chapters make the pace faster and more driving. Depending on your genre and the desired emotional impact, you'll want to use these lengths to your advantage. Varying the length and the intensity of the events within your chapters will create an engaging rhythm. Books often read like music. You need to know if you're writing a power ballad or thrash metal or a lullaby. Rises to action-packed scenes and emotional reveals should occasionally be off-set by moments of contemplation, relationship development, or preparation, allowing your reader to catch their breath before diving into the next major event.

The focus on the structure of each scene and chapter in the editing process will ensure that your structure doesn't stand in the way of your reader, but instead guides them where you want them to go in order to experience your story to its fullest.

Promises and Foreshadowing

When talking about promises in storytelling, we often refer to something called Chekhov's gun. This theory comes from the Russian author Anton Chekhov who said (I'm paraphrasing), if you set a gun on the mantel in the first act, then it absolutely must be fired by the third act. While not all books will have a literal gun, the point he was making is an important one. When you layer narrative plot devices (details and foreshadowing of events) into your manuscript, your reader will pick up on them, and in order to feel satisfied, they need a resolution on that detail. An unfired gun without a reason leaves the reader wondering why you mentioned it in the first place. With the things, people, places, events, etc. that you draw attention to, you are making promises that you will do something with them, and when you don't, the reader notices and gets frustrated. Even if the item turns out to be a red herring (a clue that leads the protagonist and the reader astray, common in mysteries) you still must resolve it in some way.

In your self-editing pass, you want to watch for these hooks and details and make sure they are resolved. Sometimes, a hook will be resolved later in the series versus in the first book. In those cases, you want to be sure the text indicates that you have not forgotten about the promise, but that you are carrying it forward. Some promises should always be resolved in each book in a series, and in a standalone novel all (Okay, maybe MOST) promises should be resolved in the end.

A Chekhov's gun is different from a McGuffin. A McGuffin is an item, event, or person that drives the plot forward, while Chekhov's gun is narrative foreshadowing. Let's look at *The Lord of the Rings* as an example. The One Ring is the McGuffin that drives the story. Frodo must take the One Ring to Mount Doom and dispose of it. This quest is the central focus of all other action. The Battle of Pelennor Fields is an interesting battle, but it is tied into keeping the focus of the Dark Lord on Gondor so the ring can move forward. It is not the point of the book. In contrast, the gifts from Lady Galadriel are Chekhov's guns. She presents them early on in the narrative, and each gift becomes important at precisely the right moment to resolve a later plot situation. When she gives Frodo the light of a star, she does so because she knows he is going into deep darkness both literally and figuratively, and that light is "fired" multiple times through the end of the series to provide a way for Frodo to survive to complete his quest.

As you review and revise your manuscript, watch for details that are laying the ground for promises and make sure these promises resolve.

STEPS TO SELF-EDITING 37

Sometimes the resolution is as simple as "hanging a lampshade" on it, which means to acknowledge the situation and give a plausible resolution without putting a lot of effort into it. This may be something like acknowledging there is a gun, but mentioning that it is so covered with rust it could never fire.

Pacing and Tension

Didn't we just talk about this? Yes, yes, we did, so this section will be short. But it's an important enough part of your self-edits that it's worth revisiting. When I talk about pacing and tension, I'm referring to how the book reads. Is it driving and fast with lots of high stakes and action? Or is it a slow discovery of love with sweeping descriptions of landscapes and verbal word play between the hero and heroine? Every book is going to have a different pace to it. This pace often is reflective of the genre, but also of the story you are trying to tell.

Within your book there are different things you can do to affect the pacing. If you want to keep the pacing quick and the tensions high, it works well to have shorter chapters and a tighter sentence structure. Often fast pacing will mean less detail, so you want to focus on making sure the details you do use have maximum effect. With a slower pace, you can delve into details and histories. You can take the time to note little details and carry themes through the entire novel. A friend of mine once said, and I think he's right, and funny, "fast pacing is the territory of exclamation points and slow pacing the territory of semi-colons."

Most novels work best when they have a balance between fast and slow. It's not an either/or, but a question of where does your novel fit on the spectrum? If everything is always high tension and action beats and running and running, your readers will get overwhelmed. Just like the characters, they need moments to catch their breath and let the emotion wane slightly so they can build to a new high. In a similar way, if the pacing is slow and wandering sometimes, we need something exciting and action packed to happen. Humor can also be used to add these up beats to a slower paced work. Because if it's always slow and meandering, the story can easily become boring. Two of the cardinal sins of authoring is when you bore a reader or confuse them, and pacing plays closely into doing those things. Too much and they're confused. Too little and they're bored.

A good way to test this is to read your book, or have an alpha reader help you by reading, and draw a red line at the point where you would stop because you are bored or confused. Figure out why that is the point where, as a reader, you'd stop reading your own book. Make corrections and then start reading again. The goal is to push the red line all the way to The End.

Point of View and Tense

Let's review, at a high level, what is meant by point of view. Point of view (POV) references how the story is told through the view point character. In fiction, the most common POVs are first and third person. These can then be further broken down into first and third person limited or broad. Also considered in POV is whether it is a singular POV or multi-POV.

First person point of view is very tight and limited to seeing only what the main character sees and what they think or feel about their situation. It is hallmarked by the use of 'I' in the telling.

For example:

I went to the store.

I staked the vampire.

My stomach rumbled with indigestion.

This POV is popular for a feeling of being right there with the character inside their head. It is very immediate, but it can be challenging as you have to figure out ways the main character would know information that they are not personally present to observe, and it is very difficult to hide surprises or reveals from the audience without the character also being surprised or unknowing. First person can be used when writing books with multiple points of view, but you need to be very cautious to label each chapter with who the first person POV is coming from and make sure each first person POV character voice is very strong. If someone picks up the book and flips it open, they should be able to tell which character is the viewpoint even if they don't look at the start of the chapter to find out.

Third person point of view is often separated into third person limited and third person broad or omniscient. In a third person POV, the usage is hallmarked by referring to the character by their name as an outside observer.

For example:

Dianna looked out over sunlit city.

Joseph readied himself for battle, drawing his sword and pounding it on his shield.

The reader is seeing the character from outside of their head, so they can often see more of what the character only observes casually or focus on the difference between what is reality and what is the character perception. In third person limited, the story is told in third person fashion, but only through the eyes of one main character, allowing you to dig deeper into their perceptions. In third person omniscient, you will have more outside observations, even though you may only have one viewpoint character. I often call this the cinematic narrator. That's the paragraphs that pop up here and there, particularly in third person, to set the scene or draw attention to the bigger world outside of the third person viewpoint character.

Third person is used very commonly when you are writing a book that has sections from many different point of view characters. Each section will be told in third person, but apply to a different character and rotate between the ensemble of characters the author has chosen. The third-person narration, in these cases, is often less confusing than having three to five first-person narrators. Having many point of view characters allows you to tell bigger stories where action may be happening in many locations that a single character can't be at, and someone coming to tell the single main character all of the information would make for a boring info dump.

In some cases, authors will combine first and third depending on the character and the timeline. As an example, I worked with an author who told everything that was happening in the now for their character in third person, but there were many flashbacks and those were all told in first person. These outlying usages *can* be effective. If done poorly or inconsistently they are confusing. It's not something I'd recommend for your first book, and you can expect that some readers won't like it, no matter how well it's done.

Other POVs include second and omniscient. These two are rarely used in fiction, though we see second person in non-fiction fairly frequently. In fact, you're seeing it now. In this point of view, the narrative voice addresses the reader as "you" and puts the reader in the place of the one having the adventure or going through the experience. So, in this book, I am addressing You as the author and the one learning.

Omniscient is a very confusing point of view, because in authors' heads it often overlaps with a multiple third person point of view, but they aren't the same. While multiple third person shows us what is going on from many point of views, we are inside of that point of view every time it is shown. Omniscient is always written in the third person, but from the point of view of an all-knowing narrator who can dip into any character at any time to give us a glimpse of what is going on in that character before moving to another. An example of this is sections of *Lord of the Rings*, particularly when the hobbits are in Mordor. During this part of the narrative Tolkien dips into the knowledge of Frodo, Sam, and several of the antagonists as needed to give the reader information and emotional flow. There was a time when omniscient storytelling was very popular in epic works, but it's not used as commonly now.

When it comes to developmental editing and point of view, you are reading to make sure the point of view is the right one to tell the story you have in mind, and that it is consistent throughout.

Now let's get a little tense. No, relax your shoulders, not that kind of tense. The tense we are talking about here is tense applied to books. Tense is a way to apply time to events. There are several grammatical tenses, but here we'll talk about the three most commonly used: past, present, and future. (If you want to get creative with them, you can learn about perfect tenses and continuous tenses from a grammar manual, but most of the time the subtypes happen naturally within the three main types.)

Past tense is used to describe an activity or event that has happened in the past. Verbs take on a past tense form, and time markers may be included to denote when the action or event took place.

Example:

Harry dove into his car and reached for his wand.

This example is happening in past tense. The story is being related to the reader from the present, denoting things that have already happened.

Present tense is used to describe an activity or event that is happening now, or a state that currently exists. The verbs take a present tense form, and time markers refer to the current moment.

Example:

Harry dives into his car and reaches for his wand.

This example happens in present tense. The story is happening in this moment. Present tense can feel more immediate and intimate to readers because they are experiencing it with the character in the moment instead of being told of something in the past.

Future tense is used to describe an event or action that is expected to happen in the future. Most books are not written fully in future tense, though some aspect of the book may be. I've seen this commonly in books where there is a prophecy or other way to consider future possibilities. The verb tense reflects this by using a future pointing helping verb before the main verb.

Example:

Harry will dive into his car and reach for his wand.

In this example, the helping verb "will" applies to both verbs "dive" and "reach" and sets them as something which is going to happen eventually, but not now.

Choosing which tense is right for your novel can be challenging. You may be guided by what is popular in your genre, or by what feels right as you create your book. There isn't a rule that all x books must be in y tense. There is a rule that you need to keep those tenses consistent throughout the book, and that's what you are looking for in your self-edit. If you find the tense keeps slipping, you need to fix it, or you may decide that the book would be better told in a different tense. That's a major revision, but happens more frequently than you might think. I always advise getting a second opinion before considering a change of that magnitude simply because of the work that goes into it. You may not change your opinion based on what anyone else says, but you may also be too close to the work to feel certain and an outside opinion may help you.

Way to Go!

THIS BRINGS US TO the end of the factors in a structural edit. This is a great time to take a deep breath and get a cookie, or a handful of carrots– we can be healthy, too. Remember not to get overwhelmed! This process gets easier with each and every self-edit, and many of the parts that I've broken out for you tie closely together. You do NOT need to reread your novel over and over again for each part of the process. Usually, the structural edit can be completed in one, maybe two, passes. Understanding the parts of the edit will make you more capable of editing for many pieces at once.

You can do this.

Now, let's move on and talk about the next editing pass where we will look at style and clarity. We'll move away from the big structure of the story, and dig into the specifics of how you're telling it.

Line or Style Editing

NOW THAT YOU'VE IDENTIFIED the big issues and made your structural edits, it's time to consider line edits. Line edits are a matter of looking at your book at the line and paragraph level. The story is solid, but is the actual process of reading the words enjoyable? Because if the reading process itself is difficult, then it doesn't matter how good the story is. Readers will stop reading.

As we talked about before, reading is all about using coded marks on a page to create in someone else's mind a picture of the people, places, and events that you want to talk about. When the words are doing their job, they almost become invisible. One of the big goals in line editing (and in copy/mechanical editing which we'll talk about in another chapter) is to make sure the text itself isn't drawing the reader's attention. You want your reader to sink into the story, not to notice that your character has blushed for the 84th time on the same page.

Another important aspect of line editing is that you are editing for audio narration. Audiobooks are a big part of our industry and that is a market that is only growing. (And the subject for another book). You want your final product to be a book that translates well to audio, and if it is awkward, repetitive, and passive, it will be difficult to narrate and hard for your audience to listen to. In some ways, creating a book that can be listened to is almost more difficult than a book that will only be read, because in reading, the human brain can make leaps and connections that don't always happen in audio. But if you make a book that reads well both to the eyes and the ears, you are expanding your market and creating a better book all together. It's very much worth the effort!

So, what factors do you want to consider in your line edit? Here are a few to focus on:

1. Eliminating wordiness and redundancy.

2. Avoiding cliches and jargon.

3. Using active voice and strong verbs.

4. Enhancing sentence structure and flow.

5. Achieving constant tone and voice.

6. Correcting for continuity.

7. Verifying point of view and tense

Like before, let's break these down.

Eliminating Wordiness and Redundancy

When it comes to identifying wordiness, there are a lot of positions that authors – and some readers– take. Some authors describe every detail and moment with the most loving and verbose language possible. Others are terse, sharp, and will never use three words where one will do the job. Technically, neither of these extremes are wrong and can be a factor in author voice and genre. However, when it comes to readability and reader engagement, there are good reasons to move toward the middle of the wordiness spectrum. When you give a reader too many words to work through, they may (probably WILL) start skimming for the "good parts." When you don't give them enough, they may become confused or bored and stop reading all together. So these corrections are all about keeping the words that are most important and increase the depth of your story and your reader engagement and letting the others go.

When you read your novel with wordiness and redundancy in mind, you want to search for repeated words and phrases and trim them away where they aren't necessary. This may mean completely removing the repetition, or tightening and shortening the phrase or sentence.

Something like:

Gertrude went to the grocery store in order to purchase everything that she needed.

can be tightened to:

Gertrude went to the grocery store to purchase cookie ingredients.

This shortens the sentence from 14 words to 10, while also using more specific language like "cookie ingredients" over "everything that she needed." Another example might be: Gertrude went to the grocery store, then she went to the hardware store, then she went to the library, and then she went to the swimming pool. This is both mechanically awkward, and it is repetitive and redundant. It could be tightened to: Gertrude went to the grocery store, the hardware store, the library, and the pool.

In trying to be precise, sometimes you can over-describe a place or an action such as: Kendal wanted to sell the old bronze fishing pole which was hanging in his garage over the freezer which meant he needed to get a stool in order to reach it. That is a very specific sentence and we can picture the rod on the wall over the freezer and the challenge to get it. But do you need all of that to get the same vision across? Can you say instead: Kendal wanted to sell the old bronze fishing pole. He'd just have to crawl over the chest freezer to get it. This is two sentences, but both are tighter writing and more active.

Be aware of prepositional phrases gone wild. Sometimes a sentence becomes overwhelmed by these phrases, usually in the search for clarity that is unnecessary because of context. We don't always have to go over the river, through the woods, up the walk, and around the hill to get to Grandma's. If you are highlighting each of those steps, why? What is the story purpose of that detail? If there is a reason for it, then leave it. If not, can we just say we're going to Grandma's house and achieve the same affect?

A similar issue is that of directionality. Do we really need to say: "He stood up."? Or is "He stood" just as strong, given that the process of standing is assumed to be in an upward direction? So, consider whether you need directors such as up, down, out to, at, etc. Sometimes they're fine, but mostly they're not necessary.

Another place where you will find a lot of repetition to consider is in character actions. Do your characters continually look, grin, shrug, smile, blink, blush, etc., etc. Every author has favorite actions that characters default to, some of them as simple as grinning, and others more complex such as eyebrow raises. It's certainly not wrong to use any of these actions, but when it's so frequent the reader could start a drinking game, you need to tone it back.

(One of my co-writers had a continually chuckling dragon. When we searched, we found nearly 70 chuckling occasions. That's one amused dragon.)

A final type of repetition to be aware of is repeated words and word sounds. Sometimes you are going for alliteration, and repeated words and word sounds are a purposeful choice. Sometimes it's just because you can't think of another way to describe an orange besides being orange. Sometimes, it's just habit. In this paragraph, I've used 'sometimes' to begin three sentences in a row. This is the kind of usage to look for and decide if the repetition is driving home a point, or if it's habit and the paragraph would read better by changing up the starting word. This happens a lot with character names or pronouns. If a whole page is full of paragraphs or sentences that start with "He verbed," or "I verbed," or "She verbed," the reading gets monotonous.

The problem with repeated sounds and syllables also applies to character names and other proper pronouns. Dr. Seuss can get away with naming his characters Thing 1 and Thing 2, but when you get into longer works, it starts getting confusing when character names all sound similar. I worked with an author once where I threatened to take away the J key on his keyboard because so many character names started with a J sound, and it was really hard to keep track of who was who. Likewise, if every character has a name that is 10 syllables long, they are all going to mush together in a reader's head and be confusing. (My husband, an avid reader, plays a mental substitution game with long or confusing character names and either shortens them to something that makes sense as a nickname, or replaces them in his head with Bob, Fred, Amy, and other short, common names. Not every reader is going to do this, but it's a good example of how readers try to deal with confusion when they really don't want to stop reading.) This doesn't mean you shouldn't name your characters appropriate to their culture or their family dynamic, just watch out when the length or the similarities become overwhelming. An easy way to do this is to create a spreadsheet with all of your proper nouns on it sorted by beginning letter or sound. If one column is overwhelming the others, considering changing around some of the names for the sake of clarity.

Line editing is where you will have to "kill your darlings", by getting rid of those phrases you love so much, but that are overused, or just don't work in context.

Avoiding Cliches and Confusing Jargon

I suppose it would be beating a dead horse, to say you should watch out for clichés and avoid them like the plague in your writing. A phrase is considered a cliché when it is overused to the point that it lacks impact and originality. Now, sometimes a cliché can be used for humor, or impact, or because it's part of a character's personality, and in those cases, you'd leave the cliché in place because it serves a purpose besides making the author giggle. (Okay, there are times to leave a cliché in place because you think it's funny, just not all the time). Search and consider and remove cliches that aren't serving a purpose or are drawing attention to the language and away from the story.

Confusing jargon falls in this same category. Jargon refers to words, abbreviations, etc. that are very specific to a character's job, culture, or surroundings. Sometimes jargon helps to establish a character, or a culture, or a genre, but when it is overused, it can simply become confusing and background noise. If you are establishing that a character is a lawyer, it may make sense to have them talk about briefs and cases and other such things, but it may be too much to have them get into the details of the law and their cases unless that is specifically relevant to the plot. One of my favorite examples of this is in the movie *Rennaisance Man* with Danny DeVito. As part of the plot, DeVito goes to work on a military base using Shakespeare to teach some of the troops. At the beginning of the work, he is utterly confused by the military speak and the abbreviations for absolutely every building on base, but by the end he is giving directions naturally using all the terms that confused him initially. This use of jargon shows the character development as he accepts the base as home. Without the ending point showing how he's changed, the jargon use would be humorous, but generally forgettable.

One last note on jargon. If you are going to use it, make sure you are using the correct words in the correct way. The difference between a clip and a magazine may not faze a general reader, but anyone who knows guns will know you're faking it if you get it wrong. Do your research!

Using Active Voice and Strong Verbs

You all knew we were going to talk about active voice versus passive voice, right? This is one of the most pounded on aspects of line editing and writing in general. When writing is passive, it slides into telling instead of showing, and throws off the pacing. Now, this is not to say that there is NEVER a place for a passive phrase or three. They can be used correctly, particularly in dialogue and non-fiction, but in most cases using active voice and strong verbs gives a sense of purpose and confidence to your writing.

Things to look for to indicate passive usage are verbs that require modifiers or help.

As an example:

I was sitting.

The action verb is "sitting." "Was" is a helping verb indicating past tense. However, you can make this action more immediate and give the verb strength by writing: I sat. The tense is correct, but the action is immediate and strong. Sat is still a common verb, so you might consider: I flopped. I collapsed. Or maybe "sat" does the job.

Could and would are other helping verbs that often indicate passive voice, and create weaker sentence structure.

I could hear the birds singing.

vs

I heard the birds sing.

vs

The damn birds sang.

vs

Birdsong blistered my ears.

Each of these phrases takes about the same amount of space on the page, but they convey very different feeling, tense, and pacing.

This is also a good time to look for filter words (we'll get into detail on these in the copy-editing section) such as: a little bit, for a moment, rather, just, very, quite, etc. These modifiers are the author equivalent of 'um', or they show author reluctance to commit to a feeling or action.

He was a little bit angry.

vs

Fury raged inside of him.

vs

He rubbed his forehead, fighting irritation.

When we are precise about a feeling or an action, it brings clarity to the reader.

Another aspect to active voice is attributing the actions correctly. If we are not careful, we end up with body parts and other inanimate objects as the focus of our action when that is not what we intend.

His eyes darted about the room.

vs

His gaze darted about the room.

vs

He studied the room.

All three are understood, but the last example has the strongest usage. I, for one, always get the giggles when it seems that body parts are roaming about on their own. Depending on your genre, body parts may literally roam on their own, so figurative eyes darting about may be confusing.

Enhancing Sentence Structure and Flow

Recently, my young daughter and I had a rousing conversation about the grammar rules, in particular she was fascinated about using semi-colons to create long sentences. She wants to use this structure all the time because it's cool. I've edited for authors who are just like my daughter. They want to try all kinds of sentence structures based on cool factor, but don't always think about what that means to a reader or a narrator.

Another example of using structure to amuse yourself, but not a great idea in a published work. I was in a class once where the instructor had written a single sentence that was grammatically correct and covered two pages, approximately 500 words. He asked us to read the sentence aloud and tell him what we thought. Despite the "correctness" of the sentence it was painfully awkward to read and much of his meaning was muddled. Later he showed us the same passage, but broken down into a cleaner structure of multiple sentences with varying lengths and structure. The second passage read more clearly, carried the pace throughout, and was much easier to read. It is good to be technically correct, but sometimes it is better to be simple and correct.

One of the easiest ways to identify awkward sentences is to read your work out loud and then listen to it. Yes, I recommend both reading and listening, as these methods of interacting with your work use different parts of your brain. If a passage makes you stumble when you read it, that's a problem. If it catches your ear when you're listening and causes confusion, that's a problem too. Both of these methods are a good last cleanup on your manuscript to help you identify problems in sentence structure and variation that affect flow or pacing. As well, you can identify small grammatical problems that can otherwise skim past your eyes or a software checker – things such as off versus of, or on versus in. You may skim over an incorrect usage or a minor typo when you are reading, but when you hear the word "off" you know it isn't "of."

Achieving Constant Tone and Voice

Let's look at the two parts of this section separately, even though you'll probably edit for them together.

When we talk about the tone of the book, we're referring to the feeling it evokes. Is it a dark and moody Gothic piece? Is it a light and fun romance? How about a grimdark fantasy? All of those feelings come from the combinations of theme, genre, events, word choice, and structure you put into the work. A lighter work will focus on lighter subjects and use shorter sentences and chapters, to keep the story moving. Subject matter and content will steer away from explicit horror and gore, and even when explicit language and sexuality is used it will feature those lighter themes. The use of language may be more comedic. Darker toned works will work in reverse. They tend toward longer sentence structure, and darker subject matter and content.

Every book and series you create will have a tone about it, and you want to stay consistent with that tone in any related work. It is very disconcerting to the reader if a light romance ends with a tragic death, for example. It feels like the author has lost control of the story, or couldn't decide what kind of story they wanted to tell.

When you are self-editing, you want to think about the themes and tone of the story you have in mind, and then make sure your language choices reflect that theme.

Now, what is this voice we're talking about? Voice has two pieces. One piece is related to the voice of the author and the other the voice of the individual characters.

When we are talking about the voice of the author, we are referring to how you specifically write and what you write about. An example of an aspect of author voice from my own work is that I rarely to never use dialogue tags. My dialogue is attached to the appropriate character based on character voice and context from character actions and setting. This isn't a wrong way to write, or necessarily a right one, but it's how I write. Understanding your author voice is very important when it comes to not allowing software or your professional editor to edit it away. There is a difference between something being wrong according to grammatical rules, and something being a preference of the author. Preference is part of voice, and you want to guard it fiercely as long as (you knew there would be an exception, didn't you?) that preference doesn't make the work inaccessible to your audience.

Author voice may also be reflective of the genre and timeframe of the book. The types of words you would use, as the author, when writing a Regency romance are going to be very different from a Contemporary romance. It throws the reader when modern words and usage appear in books that are meant to be set in another century or a faraway place. Part of your job as the author is to do your research so that your author voice enhances their engagement in the work.

The second part of voice is character voice. This refers to dialogue and how the character speaks, but it also refers to how they think. A hardened New York police detective is going to have a very different reaction to finding a dead body as compared to a young, naïve college student. Their worldviews and background should be shown in word choice, action, and reaction.

Let me take a minute here to address accents. Spelling out accents in dialogue ("Ya cannae change the laws o'physics!) is one of those hills that authors, readers, and editors will die on based on their opinion about the practice. One of the important things to remember here is that accent isn't just about those heavy changes to word pronunciation, but also word order, meaning, and usage, and often the latter two are less jarring to read and display the character voice more clearly versus spelling out the pronunciations. We live in a fortunate time as authors because there are a lot of resources we can mine for different accents and word choice including live television shows, YouTube videos, and reaching out to beta readers from the culture or location we are drawing from. When a character speaks, you should be able to tell who it is from how they speak, the words they use, and what they talk about, not only how many ways you can spell "can't."

Correcting for Continuity

This is, perhaps, the shortest section to explain but can take the longest to apply. Continuity is simply how you keep details consistent all the way through the book and, if applicable, the series. This is checking to make sure that Bob doesn't become Joe half way through the book (at least without a plot point on his name change!), and that if Sarah is allergic to strawberries, she doesn't enjoy a nice shortcake in book two without running for a antihistamine. Continuity errors creep into writing very easily, especially if a work has taken a long time to create or has been edited repeatedly. Sometimes an edit will remove a reference, and if you forget to check the rest of the book it will pop back up later.

When self-editing, we are looking for those details and making sure they are correct. This is where having a story bible or at least a few spreadsheets can be helpful. In particular, if you are dealing with items like fantasy names with strange spellings or large maps where your directions and geography must be correct, having the master resource file on hand can improve and speed up your continuity check. Many authors find that this check is best done after they've had some time away from the manuscript so that the details fade in their mind. Others lean more heavily on beta readers and professional editors to find these details as they can be difficult to see when you've been living so deeply in your story for so long. It is still an important self-editing step. You want to find these errors before your readers point them out.

Verifying Point of View and Tense

Choosing which point of view (or points of view) you are going to use in your book is usually done early on before the book is begun. In these cases, verifying the point of view is pretty straightforward. The place where point of view can become tricky to edit for are in the cases where you choose an atypical point of view (second person, anyone?), when your point of view shifts in the manuscript (usually according to rules like main character chapters in first, and secondary character chapters in third), or when you completed the manuscript in one point of view and then decided later to shift to another point of view and rewrite.

In these cases of rewritten or shifting point of view, give yourself a lot of grace for not seeing everything. Your brain has seen the whole manuscript one way and then another one, and sometimes no matter how slowly you go, or how long wait to edit, you won't see the forest for the trees. A sharp-eyed beta reader, or professional editor, more than earns their keep in making sure all the POVs are consistently changed. Unexpected, or incorrect, POV shifts is one of the things I see a lot of reader complaint about. We often call this head-hopping and try to avoid it.

Now, before someone protests, I have seen whole books written where the author drifts from one POV to another, sometimes mid-sentence, and those books sold well. It happens. Sometimes it is an aspect of omniscient point of view, and sometimes the story is so well told that readers either don't notice or don't mind the shift. Generally, don't assume that you are that author. I always keep in mind the motto (one I heard at a conference presentation from Michaelbrent Collins): bore me or confuse me and you lose me. Head-hopping and too many POV shifts can both bore and confuse the reader, so try to keep it very clear and consistent across a scene.

Tense falls into a similar category as point of view when it comes to line editing. Usually, you've chosen what tense to write in before starting the book, so the self-editing search is to make sure that each sentence is in the correct tense. If the book has been rewritten from one tense to another, or contains sections that shift tense in order to add emphasis or to show a change in scene, then your self-edit will require additional attention to detail. Again, more of these may be caught after the self-edit pass, as they can be very easy to miss.

Take a Breather

THIS WRAPS UP OUR line editing pass. Take a breather and let the information sink in. As mentioned, I'm breaking out details that you will naturally group together when you are reviewing your manuscript. You will generally only need one pass for line editing. Many professional editors will combine line editing with their developmental edits or with their copy edits. Seeing awkwardness or continuity errors can often happen at the same time as hunting for typos and improperly placed commas. A little practice and you'll see where your edits go hand in hand.

Copy or Mechanical Editing

Copy editing is what most people actually think of when they hear the word editing. Copy edits are the nitty gritty edits digging down into grammar and usage rules that many of us learned in high school and promptly forgot. Now, there are a lot of great grammar books out there (I'll put some of my favorites in the resources appendix in the back.), and I'm not going to go into lengthy grammatical explanations for everything. However, in this section I am going to dig into some of the most common grammar issues, usage mistakes, and words and phrases that always deserve a "search and consider."

Micro Versions of Line Editing Items

In the line editing section, we talked about a lot of aspects to look for and correct. In that pass, you are really working on a large, or macro, level. During your copy edit pass these issues may require further refinement on a micro level, changing one word instead of a whole section, or moving something from one place to another. I'm not going to review each of those points to avoid redundancy, but know those issues may still need tightening.

The General Typo Search

Almost every writing software out there has a spellchecker that will help you to catch general typos, and you would be surprised how often authors forget to use it. Misspellings of common words is one of the things a lot of readers notice and dislike. It's hard to trust an author to tell a good story when the manuscript is riddled with simple fat-fingered errors. So, turn on the spellcheck, track them down, and wipe them out.

Hyphenation

Hyphens (a short dash) serve as a way to join or divide words. Echoing back to those basic grammar classes, you use a hyphen to divide a compound word that spans the space between two lines in a paragraph. Fortunately, many word processors and formatting software will deal with this type of hyphenation for you. It doesn't mean you shouldn't keep an eye out for anything that looks strange. Recently, I was formatting a book and the software kept trying to hyphenate the word book to carry it across two lines, and it placed the hyphen as: boo-k. This is silly, and was an error being introduced electronically. Once I removed the word and retyped it, it moved properly to the following line. I blame electronic gremlins.

Other hyphenation cases can be words that are always hyphenated, or words that take on a hyphen based on what they are modifying. The dictionary can be a good reference for deciding if a word is hyphenated, two separate words, or a compound word. Reminder: Always use the same dictionary for all of your books in a series, so that the rules you are following remain consistent. Believe it or not, all dictionaries don't match, so you want to choose one and stick with it.

Examples of commonly hyphenated words:

- Father-in-law

- Editor-in-chief

- Six-pack

- Long-term

When spelled out, we also hyphenate numbers from 21-99.

- Twenty-one

- Eighty-two

Prefixes "ex", "self", and "all" also call for a hyphenation:

- The villagers believed the wizard was all-knowing.

- Her ex-husband had fallen into a ditch.

- Learning the art of meditation can increase self-confidence.

One of the hardest hyphenation decisions is when you are dealing with words that are hyphenated when they are acting as close adjectives, but are not hyphenated when they follow the verb or when they are serving as nouns.

Here's an example:

Correct:

Despite being stuffed with onions and oranges, the Thanksgiving turkey was bone dry.

Also Correct:

Buddy made a bone-dry turkey.

Incorrect:

The turkey was bone-dry.

You can test to see if the adjectival form is hyphenated based on being placed near the noun it is modifying and then asking if the two words can modify the noun when they aren't combined. In the example, a turkey can be dry, but it can't be bone. So in order for bone-dry to work it has to be hyphened.

Be especially careful with this type of hyphenation when dealing with age.

Correct:

The 18-year-old male was late for his test.

Also correct:

My son is 21 years old.

We also hyphenate the phrase when it is used as a noun.

Correct:

This is a birthday party for 3-year-olds.

If the modifier is partnered with an -ly adverb do not use a hyphen.

Correct:

The class was given randomly assigned tests.

Incorrect:

The tests were randomly-assigned.

I completed a randomly-assigned test.

The Em-dash

So while we're taking dashes, let's take a minute to talk about the em-dash. An em-dash is a punctuation mark which looks like a long hyphen, like this —. Em-dashes have a few general uses, and are a favorite punctuation mark for some authors.

Em-dashes can be used in a sentence to set off a clause. The em-dash visually is more of a break than a comma, and more strongly sets off a clause in a situation where either paired commas or paired em-dashes are both acceptable. Likewise, em-dashes can replace parenthesis for setting off a clause.

Here are three examples, all of which are correct:

After presenting at the conference, including six presentations and four panels, Jadelynn was exhausted.

After presenting at the conference (including six presentations and four panels), Jadelynn was exhausted.

After presenting at the conference—including six presentations and four panels—Jadelynn was exhausted.

If the clause comes at the end of the sentence, you only use one em-dash.

Jadelynn was exhausted after presenting at the conference—including six presentations and four panels.

You can see how the em-dash is visually stronger, though all cases are correct.

The em-dash can also be used in dialogue to show when someone has been cut off mid-word.

"You can't go in there! By order of the qu—"

Another place em-dashes can be used is instead of a colon proceeding a list.

Let's go where we went last year—Disneyland, Lego World, and the beach.

Just keep in mind that because the em-dash is visually very bold, it can draw attention to itself in a way that takes away from the narrative.

Commas

The humble comma is one of the most used, and abused, punctuation marks in writing. They have the most guidelines, and the most exceptions to said guidelines, of any punctuation. I am not going to cover all the comma rules here. If I did, I would definitely miss one or twelve. Instead, we'll go over some of the most common situations.

Use commas in a short list.

I went to get eggs, milk, bread, and butter.

Keeping the comma before the conjunction is called the Oxford comma and is a subject of lengthy debate. Editors either love or revile the Oxford comma, but as it has been the deciding factor in a number of legal cases, it's just as well to leave it in place. You would *not* use an Oxford comma if the final two items are a single item or group.

Use commas to join two independent clauses with a conjunction.

Correct with a comma:

Bertrand knew he had to catch the thief, but he didn't know the thief wanted to catch him.

Correct without a comma:

Bertrand knew he had to catch the thief but didn't know how.

In the second case, there is not an independent clause after the conjunction so no comma is used. A good test is to read the clause on either side of the conjunction and see if it is a complete thought. If it is, then add the comma before the conjunction.

Use commas after an introductory phrase.

Sometimes we begin a sentence with a phrase to introduce the topic before completing the subject of the sentence. In these cases, use a comma to set off the introductory phrase.

In these cases, use a comma to set off the introductory phrase.

Use commas to set off a parenthetical phrase or interrupter.

This usage came up in the last section when we were discussing em-dashes. Commas can be properly used to set off a parenthetical phrase within a sentence.

The conference, which had only been established this year, was awesome!

Do not fret if you don't get all the commas in the right place. This is another situation where getting assistance will help. For all that I can see missing commas in someone else's work, I am terrible at seeing them in mine. My editor tells me that she gets out a box of commas for my edits and sprinkles them liberally.

Common Comma Mistakes

Too Few or Too Many

Commas serve as a pause or break in a sentence that is shorter than a period. When you only rely on that general guide, it is very easy to fall into the camp of the over comma or the under comma. Sometimes it helps to read a phrase out loud, or ask someone else to read it to you, and listen to where the natural pauses happen in the reading. This can help guide comma use, or help you see where too many commas are breaking the flow of the reading.

Comma Splices

It is a common temptation to use commas to join two clauses that are not independent clauses and/or do not have a conjunction.

Incorrect:

Dianna ran out of the office and down the street, she was sure she could catch the train.

In this case, the comma is splicing together two independent clauses without a conjunction. This would be more properly punctuated with a semi-colon (if the clauses are closely related), or by adding a period and creating two sentences.

Sometimes, one can argue in favor of a comma splice if the two independent clauses are very short and very closely related.

I knew I was right, I just knew it.

But you need to be consistent and, even in these cases, consider using the full stop punctuation.

Numbering

Let's back away from the punctuation, you can find more details in your favorite grammar guide, and talk about some more general usage. When it comes to numbering in your manuscript there are some good rules to know.

- Spell out numbers from one to ninety-nine. Numbers 100 or more are written numerically. If you have two numbers in a sentence follow the rule for each.

  ○ When I turned four, I got 100 presents.

- If you have more than two numbers in a sentence apply the rule of the majority.

  ○ The lottery numbers were: 100, 101, 102, and 4.

- If you are using numbers that are over three digits, don't forget the comma.

- 1,000

- Time can be expressed in a number of ways.

  - 5:00 am, 5:00 a.m. (the periods are most commonly used in fiction, again be consistent).

  - 5 o'clock

  - Five-thirty

- When you refer to height, you rarely hyphenate the number.

  - Six foot four (This is the exception to the rule if it is modifying a noun, in which case it is hyphenated as per the rules discussed above.)

  - Six feet four inches

  - 6'4"

- In reference to money follow the hyphenation rules for adjectives, and use the numerical reference to create a specific amount.

  - He had a hundred-dollar bill.

  - There were one hundred dollars.

  - $724.88

- When it comes to years, particularly in a citation or when creating a bibliography, use the format recommended by your style guide. In other cases, there are a number of ways to represent the date. Be aware that in the United States dates are represented as month/day/year, but it is day/month/year almost everywhere else.

- 5 Mar 2020

- March 4th 2020

- 3/4/2020

- Spell out numbers in dialogue except for common instances like 911.

- When referring to the floors of a building, Floor 4 or 4th floor are both correct.

Dialogue Punctuation

Correctly punctuating dialogue can be tricky, and it's a subject that we could devote a lot of electronic ink to. For this discussion, we'll touch on the basics.

- Begin and end dialogue with quotation marks.

"Let's all go to the movies."

- Use a comma to introduce dialogue when the introduction is not a complete sentence.

Master Ludwig said, "Beware the evil eye."

- Use commas when a quotation is interrupted by a dialog tag.

"What the king dreams," Alan said, "the Hounds create."

- Use a colon or a period when the dialogue is proceeded by a complete sentence.

Dianna flopped on the couch and covered her eyes with her arm. "There's food in the fridge. Take what you want."

- Leave quotations open in dialogue with several paragraphs. This means you will start with a quotation mark at the beginning of the first paragraph, but not add one at the end of the paragraph. The next paragraph will also begin with a quotation mark, but the ending quotation mark is not put in place until the dialogue belonging to the same person ends.

"Welcome to the deepest darkest jungle.

"We will work together to hunt down and destroy the Breath of Evil.

"Any questions?"

- Use single quotes when your dialogue is quoting someone else.

"I promise that's what he said. 'Winter is coming.'"

Dialogue Tags

Now that we know how to punctuate common dialogue, let's talk about dialogue tags. A dialogue tag is the bit that comes at the end, or the beginning, or the middle and states who is talking. For example: Jana said.

You use these tags in the dialogue to create clarity about who is speaking. There are a few schools of thought about dialogue usage that you should be aware of.

1. Keep it simple and use only said or asked, as these tags are invisible to the reader.

2. Said is dead! Use expressive tags. Shout, clamor, exclaim, tell.

3. Kill off dialogue tags and use actions or character voice within the dialogue to indicate who is speaking.

Contrary to popular belief, none of these options is completely wrong. This is one of the many issues that comes down to being consistent, and not letting the words get in the way of the story. For example, when you choose a dialogue tag like "ejaculated," the reader is going to pay a LOT more attention to the tag than to the dialogue. If there are no tags or actions at all, the dialogue reads like two heads talking in a white room, and unless there really are two heads talking in a white room, you want to add to that scene. So figure out your style, and then be consistent with the usage.

The one thing almost everyone agrees on is avoiding the use of what are commonly called Tom Swifties (this was coined by *Boy's Life Magazine*) dialogue tags, which is when you are using -ly adverbs to modify dialogue tags, particularly when the -ly adverb is a wordplay on a term in the dialogue.

"I hate it when zombies rise at the morgue." Jay said morbidly.

Better options:

"I hate it when that happens." Jay grumped.

Or

Jay scrambled to catch the drink, but it fell over anyway. "I hate it when that happens."

Or

"Dangit! I hate it when that happens."

Every option is better than morbidly.

-ly Adverbs

An adverb is a word or phrase that modifies an adjective, verb, or another adverb or word group. Many adverbs end in the suffix -ly, and are identified as adverbs because of that construction. Like other situations we've talked about, writers and readers are highly divided over the use of adverbs. They are easy shorthand to modify a word; however, it's often better to use a stronger verb or line of action over the -ly verb.

Sable was extremely hungry.

Or

Sable was ravenous!

The stronger verb creates a better mental picture and tone.

Use -ly adverbs the way you use anchovies on pizza, with a gentle hand, or not at all.

When it comes to other adverbs, this advice also applies. Adverbs such as "very", "really", "rather", and "quite" are redundant modifiers.

Is a man very angry or is he furious?

Is the school really far away, or is it miles away?

The place where these modifiers have a strong place is in dialogue, in particular when you are writing a younger character, or if they are particular to a certain dialect or region.

Mark Twain's advice on this subject was, "Substitute "damn" every time you're inclined to write "very", your editor will delete it and the writing will be just as it should be."

Filler Words

There are a number of words that are referred to as filler words, meaning they fill space, but don't actually do much. These words are the authorial equivalent of saying "um". Other times they represent being unwilling to commit to an action, feeling, or setting. Using these words occasionally isn't a problem, but when they appear again and again, they take away strength from your prose and weaken your author voice. So always "find and consider" these words. Remove the ones that aren't doing the job, and leave the rest.

Also know that every author has their favorite filler words or go to actions. I'll give you a list here to start with, but add to this list with words and phrases you identify as your unique, repetitive go tos.

Filler words and overuse:

- Directional words related to obvious action. Up, down, left, right, etc.

  ○ He sat down on the chair. – The down is unnecessary because how else is he going to sit? If you are writing in a genre where the direction isn't obvious without the filler word, then go ahead and add it.

- Always and never. These are absolutes, so you need to consider whether they are correct. Does Dave really NEVER shave? Or does he just put it off because he's lazy?

- Stuff and things. These are perfectly nice words, but don't really tell the reader much. "Jacob got his stuff and left" is not very specific. "Jacob made a peanut butter sandwich and drove to work" paints a more specific picture.

- That. Grammatically the word "that" is used to indicate a specific object, item, person, etc. and is used to introduce a restrictive clause. The word "which" is used to introduce a non-restrictive clause. If you have a restrictive clause, you may be able to remove "that." The rule, particularly in informal settings, is if the meaning is not altered by removing "that," you can remove it.

- Think, thought, felt, feel, realize, wonder. These are all words that tell the reader what the character is experiencing. This falls under the advice to show instead of tell. Can you give your reader a deeper experience by saying, "Susan's eyes pricked with tears and her stomach ached", instead of "Susan felt sad"? You don't have to over do this, but you should consider your options.

- Went. This is another word that doesn't tell us much. "George went to the store." It's nice. It's fine. It's boring. "George raced to the store on his Harley." Much more evocative.

- Just. Just is another wimpy modifier.

  ○ Everything is just fine. Vs. Everything is great.

- Irregardless. Irregardless means the same as regardless, and is considered a nonstandard or nonsensical word. It has a place in dialogue, as people use nonstandard words all the time, but consider carefully its place anywhere else. Particularly in non-fiction or formal fiction, the use should be regardless.

- Then in series. "Then" is often misused to link together several actions. I went to the store, then I went home, then I unloaded the groceries, then I put them away, then I took a nap. This is a convoluted way to link the actions together. Moving away from the "then" list can make for a clearer structure and more detail. I went to the store, then home, where I unloaded the groceries and put them away. All of my jobs done, I took a nap.

- Start, begin, began, begun. When a verb is started or begun there is an underlying expectation that the action will be interrupted. If the action isn't interrupted, then the indication of starting or beginning is unnecessary.

I began to walk to the door. (And then what? This is awkward unless something happens next.)

I walked to the door. (Strong verb, easy to follow the action.)

He started to kiss her, but she jerked back and slapped his face. (Here the started action is suspended by the response.)

- Overused actions: look, breathe, shrug, nod, chuckle. Just about anything can be an overused action. I personally overuse lip licking and grinning in my prose and have to search for those in my edits.

- Over-the-top adjectives. Amazing! Fascinating! Incredible! Marvelous! Stunning! Surprising! Unbelievable! Astounding! Miraculous! Mind-blowing! Staggering! Wonderful! These are all acceptable words, but make sure you are using them where they belong. Books written with younger protagonists may use such words more often, especially in dialogue. Overuse of big adjectives can make your book sound trite or like a golden-age comic book. Save these for the right moment, and make it count.

Often-Confused Words

An entire book could be dedicated to words which are close in spelling and sound, but very different in meaning, that are often improperly used, but we'll just hit some of the most common ones here.

- Accept/except – Accept is an action/Except means to leave something out

- Loose/lose – Loose with two os means slack/lose with one o means to fail

- Lead/led – Lead is an irregular verb meaning to show the way. The past tense of lead is led.

- Further/farther – Further means to a degree or extent. "I wanted to discuss the mission further." Father is literal distance. "He lives farther away than his brother."

- Fewer/less – Fewer is used to denote things that can be counted. If it can't be counted use less. I have fewer cookies than my brother. I have less time than I thought.

- Its/it's – Its shows ownership/it's is the conjunction of it is.

- There/they're/their – There shows place/they're is the contraction of they are/their shows possession

- Lay/laid/lie – Lay and lie are present-tense verbs, but have different meanings. Lay means to put something down, so the subject has to act upon the object. Example: I lay down the book. Lie means to stay or rest in a horizontal position. So you lie down to sleep, because you are the subject and you are acting on yourself, not another object. This becomes confusing when you are the subject and the object in the sentence, such as in the opening of the child's pray where it is written "Now I lay me down to sleep", but that's correct because you have both a subject and an object. The past tense lay becomes laid. Lie becomes lay, and when helping verbs get in the mis lay becomes laid and lie becomes lain. (Note: this set of words is my personal bane. I have a chart from

Grammar Girl that I printed up and put near my computer. I check it every time. There is no shame in not remembering any of these rules by heart.)

- You're/your/yore – You're is the contraction of you are/your shows possession/yore is an ancient point in time.

Also related to incorrect usage are homonyms and homophones. Homonyms are words that have the same spelling but different meanings or pronunciations. Homophones are words with the same sounds and/or spelling but different meanings. And let's be honest, you don't have to know the difference. You do need to be able to identify when you are using the right word when two words sound the same but have different meanings. Here are some examples of commonly misused homophones and homonyms. A spell checker will not find these because they are not misspellings, but they may be the wrong word in context.

Homophone Examples:

- Bare/bear – Uncovered/a large mammal

- Baring/bearing – To "bare" make uncovered/to "bear" or withstand

- Bolder/boulder – More bold or thicker/a big rock or a larger rock

- Canon/cannon – An accepted principle, rule or backstory/a large gun

- Cell/sell – A small room found in a prison, a small unit in biological function/to exchange a product or service for money

- Cite/sight/site – A reference in a report, book, or other location/seen with the eyes or vision/a location

- Creak/creek – A sound/a small stream of water

- Dew/do/due – small water droplets that gather on plants and surfaces overnight/a verb indicating action/deadlines or a time when an event is going to happen

- Flour/Flower – Ground wheat/The blossom of a plant, to open up

- Hi/high – A common greeting, short for Hello/at great height, a measurement of height

- Hole/whole – An opening in something/complete

- Incite/insight – To rile up or encourage/to see the inner nature

- Idle/idol – Lazy or without motivation/someone or something you admire or worship

- Know/No – To have knowledge/negative, opposite of yes

- Lessen/lesson – To reduce/a period of learning or learning plan

- Meet/meat – Encounter someone or something for the first time/animal flesh

- Pair/pear/pare – Two of an item/a type of fruit/to cut with a small knife

- Peak/peek/pique – Maximum height or top/a quick look/getting one's interest

- Pray/prey – A form or worship/something hunted

- Hawk/hock – A large bird/to sell wares or services

- Rain/reign/rein – A weather phenomenon, water that falls from the sky/to rule/a leather strap often used with animals

- Real/reel – Genuine/a holding device that items such as string, yarn, or film is wrapped around

- Role/roll – A person's place and position, or a part they act/action of rolling, a type of food

- Sale/sail – A discounted cost on an item or service/part of a boat or ship

- Sole/soul – Having to do with the foot/the spirit or emotional nature of people

- Stare/stair – To look at something intently/rising levels between two floors of a building

- Stationary/stationery – Staying still, in one spot/papers and envelopes

- Steal/steel – To take something without permission/a type of iron based metal

- Tail/tale – The back end of a creature, something that follows you/a story

- Waist/waste – Part of the body/discard or overuse

- Weak/week – Not strong/the duration of seven days, usually denoted Monday-Sunday

- Wear/where – To put on/a place

Homonym Examples:

- Bass – A species of fish/a type of stringed instrument

- Bright – Intelligent or smart, quick witted/filled with light

- Bow – An accessory made from ribbon or other material/to bend the body

- Close – Nearby/to shut an opening

- Current – A point in time, now/an electrical measurement

- Does – A group of female deer/to do something

- Dove – A white bird or bird species/past tense of dive

- Fly – A small insect/to hover above the ground

- Kind – Of a type/caring or gentle

- Match – To put two like things together/a wooden stick with a chemical tip meant for starting fires

- Record – A piece of evidence about the past/to film something with technology

- Ring – To call someone on the telephone or cellphone/a band worn on the finger or toes

- Right – Correct/the opposite of left

- Rose – To rise up/a type of flower

- Sow – Female pig/to plant a seed

- Spring – A season/a coiled object

- Tear – A rip in an object/droplets that fall from the eyes

- Well – A feeling of contentment/a deep hole from which water is drawn

- Wind – Movement of air/to wrap around something

- Wound – An injury/past tense of wind

The terms here are certainly not all of the possibilities, but should give you some good examples. If in doubt, check the dictionary and make sure you have chosen the correct spelling and usage in the context of your manuscript.

Passive Voice and Showing vs Telling

We've mentioned both of these issues before, but your copy-editing pass is a final chance to search for places where the voice is not strong or is relying too much on telling and not enough showing. Remember that passive voice may be properly used in dialogue, and will appear more in formal writing and non-fiction. It is not automatically wrong to use passive voice, or to tell instead of show, but you need to watch for how these things affect the depth of your writing and the pacing. Most of the time removing these issues will create a better reader experience.

Reminder of things to look for:

Passive voice:

- Helping verbs

    ○ Helping verbs + an -ing verb

        • The Brown Family was driving to church.

        • The Brown Family drove to church.

    ○ Helping verbs + action verb

        • I could hear the birds chirping.

            ○ I heard the birds sing.

- I can remember the song.

  ○ I remembered the song.

- When the subject is acted on by the object.

  ○ The boy was bitten by the dog. – Passive.

  ○ The dog bit the boy. – Active

Showing versus telling:

- Search for words such as felt, knew, thought, etc.

- Search for the word 'was'. Often was is a telling indicator.

  ○ I was sad.

  ○ I wiped away my tears, my chest heavy.

  ○ The dog was happy.

  ○ The dog's tail wagged, and it spun in place when it saw the girl.

Reading Like a Reader

Now that you've completed your revisions, there is one more critical read through to complete. This one may require setting the manuscript aside for a day or two so you can clear your mind, because the last read has nothing to do with making corrections or remembering technical grammatical advice, and at this point you may be *very* sick of your book. This last pass is reading as a reader. Turn off your editorial brain and take a look at what you've accomplished. Read for the joy of it. At the end ask yourself the following questions:

1. Was the book interesting?

2. Did it flow well or did it bog down?

3. Were you ever lost or confused?

4. Were you ever bored?

5. Would you read another book from you?

If you're not satisfied by your answers to these questions, there's more work to do.

Helpful Methods to Make Self-Editing Easier

WHEN YOU ARE DEEP in revisions, you can end up feeling blinded by all the words and all the rules. There are some techniques you can try to see if they help your self-editing experience.

- Print out a hard copy and mark it up with a red pen. Working on paper instead of electronically works particularly well for visual and tactile learners. This can be expensive if you have a really big book. You may want to consider having it printed at a shop with a laser printer.

- Change the font style and size. In my opinion, this is the only purpose for Comic Sans font. It is such a big visual change that your brain can't skip over words.

- Read your work backwards. Yes, this is a thing. Start at the end and read one paragraph or even one sentence at a time, going backwards. This is particularly helpful in your copy-editing pass when you don't want to get drawn into the narrative, but only want to focus on each passage at a micro level.

- Read your work out loud. The process of reading the work makes you look at every word. This is particularly helpful in identifying small errors with similar words such as "on" versus "in" or "of" versus "off". Visually, these errors are easy to skim over, but when you read the work out loud you will hear where it's wrong.

- Have someone read your work to you. There are a number of apps that will do this if you don't have a convenient human around. As above, the process of listening can show you small errors. It can also point out areas of awkward phrasing or repetitive issues you haven't noticed.

Perfection is the Enemy of Done

It comes as no surprise that revisions and editing are not most authors' favorite part of creating a book. (Some authors adore editing their own word, and I tip my hat to them.) Most of us want to finish one book and get on to the next one! There is so much excitement in the creating, that the prospect of shining and polishing it is daunting. Take heart.

There are professionals who will tell you that all of this revising and editing is a waste of time. Write once, get it proofread, publish it. In my experience, this advice comes from professionals who have been in the industry for a while and have a lot of books under their belt. They've practiced and revise and cycle naturally as they create, so their "rough draft" isn't nearly as rough as a first draft from a new writer. The other source of this advice is people who are very aware of financial issues around editing and don't believe it is necessary. You have to figure out where you are in your career and your quality before embracing this method. Quality issues get books removed from distributors and gather bad reviews.

I mentioned early on, and I'm going to repeat it now, that you need to find a balance between doing too little and doing too much. Self-editing is your pass before sending your manuscript to an agent or to a professional editor (at the *very* least a proofreader), so there will be one more chance for errors to get cleaned up. And even if a few errors get through (they totally will), you can make minor corrections to your work over time. Do not be a perfectionist. Perfection is the enemy to done, and too many editing passes can squash your author voice and waste your time. Set yourself a limit, I suggest one to three passes, do your best and be done.

Finding an Editor

You've done everything we've talked about. Your manuscript is just as pretty as you can make it, and you're ready for the next step. Congratulations!!!

Now what?

Now it's time to find an editor. There are a few things to consider before doing so.

One of the biggest things you need to determine is what kind of editing you need. You just learned the three types of editing: developmental, line, and copy. Professional editors will usually specialize in either developmental and line, or line and copy. Not many editors do only line editing. It fits too naturally with developmental or copy so tends to get bundled.

I know editors, and authors, who insist that every book should have self-edits, and then a professional editor for developmental, and one for copy, and one for proofreading. (We haven't talked much about proofreading yet because it is the final step before publication and isn't done in a self-edit.) I am not in this camp. I think every author is different and will need different things for different stages of their career and for different books.

Early in your career, you may need more editing assistance at the developmental level, but as you mature in your writing and develop connections with good beta readers, that need may drop off.

You may also have some books that require a content expert or sensitivity reader, which are not types of edits, but are services some editors or specialists offer. A content expert is someone with specialized knowledge about a particular field or time period. Authors who write historical fiction, for example, may need someone to verify that their fashion descriptions are correct for the historical period. A sensitivity reader will read for appropriate depictions of a special group or type of people.

So how do you choose what you need? Unfortunately, I can't tell you exactly what goes into that decision. I can suggest that giving your book to a beta reader after your self-edit may help. If your reader has a lot of general confusion about the plot and characters, or the logical flow and lessons in non-fiction, then you need developmental assistance. If your beta's questions are for specific word usage and typos, you need a copy editor, or a strong proofread.

You want an editor who knows your genre. It's not impossible for a romance editor to edit a fantasy book, but they won't have the understanding of the tropes and expectations and specific details of your genre and that leads to a weaker edit.

Your finances will also come into play here. Top level editors with a lot of experience who are offering a lot of services will be more expensive. Editing is generally charged by the word and very experienced editors will often charge $0.03-0.05 per word (USD). That means a 100,000 word manuscript can run \$3,000-\$5,000 in editing. Newer editors may charge as little as \$0.006-0.008 per word for developmental edits and \$0.005-0.008 per word for copy edits as they are building their portfolio and experience. These ranges make authors crazy, and I wish we had a better process for determining who charges what.

Many editors will ask for a sample of your writing, and may even edit that sample for free or for a reduced rate. The reason for this is for both the editor's and your benefit. The editor gets to see your style and can estimate how much work the full manuscript is going to be, and you get to see what their editorial style is like and if you connect well. Personally, I charge less for working on a very clean manuscript over one I can see from the get-go is going to take a lot of time and be very difficult work.

In your authoring life, you'll probably try a few editors before you find the one that meshes with you in terms of understanding your genre, your writing, and your goals while being someone you can afford. Once you find that editor, hang onto them!

Places you can go to find an editor:

- Reedsy – Reedsy is an online option where you can look at the portfolios of freelance editors and hire them. It's a great site with top level talent, but typically it's expensive talent.

- Upwork – Like Reedsy, Upwork is an online gathering of freelancers where you can post a job you need to have done and get responses, or invite an editor to work with you. There is more variety here and editors with a range of experience and prices. The pro of working through someplace like Upwork over working directly with an editor is that the company handles contracts and disputes.

- Agencies – These are editorial companies with a stable of editors who have been vetted and trained by the company. You work with the company who assigns you an editor and monitors the process with them. Some of the companies that I have worked with:

  ○ The Manuscript Doctor

  ○ Eschler Editing

  ○ Salt and Sage

- Facebook Groups – There are a lot of Facebook groups for helping authors connect with author services. Make sure you follow the rules of the group, whatever they may be. Often authors will put up a post with their genre and needs and ask other authors to recommend their editors or editors to leave links to their social media pages or websites.

- Private Freelance websites – If you do a Google search for freelance editors, you will find any number of websites. Make sure you read the fine print as you reach out to freelance editors and absolutely get a contract. Not just an email of agreement to work on the book, but an honest to goodness contract that states what work will be done, in what time frame, at what cost. It should include terms for cancellation and many will also have a non-disclosure agreement (NDA) to protect your story from being shown to others.

- Conferences – Many editors attend writing conferences and will be happy to give you a business card and talk about what they can do. Some conferences even have a free editing table or a vendor room where you can get a sample edited and meet local editors.

A final concern I'm going to talk about. There have been a few documented cases of editors taking author's stories and selling them as their own or sharing them with others. This is a case of a few bad apples making people doubt the barrel. I cannot say this never happens. I can say that it's very, very rare. As an author, I never worry about my editor taking off with my books or my ideas—any editor involved in such behavior could get away with it once before no one would give them any other books—but this is also why I so strongly encourage you to have a contract. If something feels wrong, get out of the relationship.

In Conclusion

WELL, HERE WE ARE at the end of our long self-editing talk. I truly hope that the information in this book is useful to you, and maybe sets some of your worries at ease. It is a wonderful time to be an author. You have more options for getting your work out into the public than ever before, but it's critical that the work you put out is high quality that represents your author brand well and brings readers back for more. Learning to self-edit your books is an effort that is well worth the time, and will save you time, frustration, and money.

Now it's time for you to get back to work. Pack up some of the virtual cookies. I'll make more. You're welcome back any time, and if you have questions that I haven't answered here, feel free to contact me at .

Resources

DICTIONARY

Merriam Webster Dictionary

Oxford English Dictionary

Non-Fiction Style Guides

MLA

APA

Fiction Style Guides

Chicago Manual of Style Seventeenth Edition (also available online at www.chicagomanualofstyle.org)

Grammar Guides

Grammar Girl – www.quickanddirtytips.com/grammar-girl

Conan the Grammarian by Susan Mackay Smith

Beat and Structure Guides

Save the Cat Writes a Novel by Jessica Brody

Romancing the Beat by Gwen Hayes

Writing into the Dark by Dean Wesley Smith

The Story Grid by Shawn Coyne

Bird by Bird by Anne Lamott

Eats, Shoots, and Leaves by Lynne Truss

Other helpful books

Self-Editing for Fiction Authors by Renni Browne and Dave King

The Emotional Thesaurus by Becca Puglisi and Angela Ackerman

Definitions for Editing Terms and Abbreviations

- Artificial Intelligence (AI) – Computer programs capable of generating art and the written word. Also capable of some level of editing, translation, transcription and other services. Most AI currently on the market is not truly Intelligent but is a Large Language Model (LLM) based on a huge database from which it can extrapolate and recombine information.

- Chekov's gun – A narrative device to foreshadow an action or event later in the book.

- Copy Edit (CE) – A manuscript revision based on addressing grammatical issues, typos, and detailed fixes.

- Developmental Edit (DE) – A manuscript revision based on addressing large structural and developmental issues such as character arcs, plotting problems, etc.

- Fiction – Prose that describes fictional people and events.

- Head hopping – Switching between points of view without a

scene break or chapter.

- Intellectual property (IP) – Not only the manuscript you create, but the specifics of characters, settings, etc. There are limits to what you can call your specific IP guided by the law, but much of what goes into your manuscript is your intellectual property. Guard it fiercely.

- Kindle Direct Publishing (KDP) – Amazon's publishing arm where you can upload e-book or print on demand files.

- Line Edit (LE) – Manuscript revision focused on the flow of the language. Meant to fix repetition and awkwardness over specific grammar.

- McGuffin – An object, person, or idea that drives a plot. All other action revolves around solving the issues related to the McGuffin.

- Non-fiction – Prose that is based on facts, real events, and real people.

- Point of View (PoV or POV) – The viewpoint from which a manuscript or section of a manuscript is told.

- Professional Editing/Editor – Hiring a trained professional to edit a manuscript.

- Proofread – The final pass through a manuscript following acceptance of all editing material to look for typos or formatting errors.

- Self-Editing – Author editing of their own work

- Self-Publishing – Author production and sales of a manuscript or other IP.

Average Word Count Information

IN PUBLISHING, WE TALK about word count and not page count because how many words fit on a page varies too much. Anyone who has had a college assignment based on page count has probably pulled the stunt of messing with margins or font size to force too little text to fill all of the space. As well, a page in a 6x9 inch book isn't going to hold the same number of words as a page in an 8x5.5 inch book. Then you have e-readers that allow the font sizes to be changed on the fly. So, what is represented on a page is crazy inconsistent. Thus wordcounts.

The lists here are mostly applicable to traditional publishing, though it's not a bad thing for self-published authors to consider these numbers as good guidelines anyway, particularly on a first publication. It is great advice to use as many or as few words as the story needs to tell it in a satisfying way, but there are reader expectations to think about too. Just because you think the story needs a million words doesn't mean anyone will agree to read that many. What these numbers really represent is a way to look at your marketing and your reader expectations as well as the expectations from agents and editors.

General Guidelines

Emphasis on the word **guidelines**. People argue these counts all the time, but like other lists in this book, this will give you a good starting place.

Flash fiction: 100-1500 words

Short Story: 1500-7,500 words

Novelette: 7,500-17,500 words

Novella: 17,500-40,000 words

Novel: Over 40,000 though most novels average 50,000-90,000 words

Epic novel: Over 110,000 words

Average Wordcount By Genre

Nonfiction

Memoir: 45,000-80,000 words

Standard Nonfiction/Commercial Novels: 30,000-70,000 words

How-to/Self-Help: 40,000-50,000 words

Biography: 80,000-200,000 words

Fiction Genres

Fantasy: 50,000-150,000 words

Science Fiction: 50,000-150,000 words

Historical Fiction: 80,000-120,000 words

Romance: 40,000-90,000 words

Chick Lit: 70,000-75,000 words

Women's Fiction: 80,000-90,000 words

Mystery/Crime: 40,000-80,000 words

Thriller/Suspense: 40,000-100,000 words

Horror: 40,000-80,000 words

Dystopian: 60,000-100,000 words

Western: 50,000-80,000 words

Young Adult: 60,000-90,000 words

Children's Books

Picture Books: 100-800 words

Early Readers: 200-3500 words

Chapter Books: 4000-10,000 words

Middle Grade: 20,000-55,000 words

About the Author

JANA S. BROWN FELL in love with reading and writing when she was very young. She studied editing and publication in college and started work as an editor and Executive Secretary for *The Leading Edge – Magazine of Science Fiction and Fantasy* in the mid 1990s. She's spent the last 30ish years working as an editor, author, technical writer, presenter, and marketer.

Come and visit her website at www.opalkingdompress.com and join her newsletter for release announcements, sneak peeks and prizes.

Want to learn more from Jana? Visit www.geekgirlsacademy.com for courses, references, and author community!

Acknowledgements

I've never had a book go out into the wild without a lot of help, but this book in particular owes its existence to some amazing people. In the summer of 2023, I had major back surgery and was left with a lot of brain fog while I recovered. It was a struggle to even try to sit down and write, but encouragement from Melissa Proffitt, Bryan Brown, Lyn Worthen, Jodi Milner, and Wendy Christensen in particular kept me coming back and putting the words on the page. Thank you so much.

www.ingramcontent.com/pod-product-compliance
Lightning Source LLC
Chambersburg PA
CBHW050537280326
41933CB00011B/1617